MW01491202

the Lost
Treasures
OF GENESIS

NATHANIEL T. JEANSON

INSTITUTE FOR
CREATION
RESEARCH

Dallas, Texas
www.icr.org

After receiving his Ph.D. in cell and developmental biology from Harvard Medical School in 2009, Dr. Nathaniel Jeanson joined ICR as a Research Associate. While at Harvard, he assisted in adult stem cell research, specifically on the role of Vitamin D in regulating blood stem cells. Dr. Jeanson has a B.S. in Molecular Biology and Bioinformatics from the University of Wisconsin-Parkside, where his research efforts involved working with single-cell algae to decipher molecular mechanisms of plant function. Additionally, he has submitted testimony to the Massachusetts governing bodies in opposition to human embryonic stem cell research and has been a panelist at the Massachusetts Citizens for Life convention. As Deputy Director for Life Sciences, Dr. Jeanson's current research at ICR involves the investigation of molecular mechanisms of biological change from a young-earth perspective. He also serves as a member of the Master Faculty of ICR's School of Biblical Apologetics. He regularly contributes research articles to ICR's monthly magazine *Acts & Facts*.

THE LOST TREASURES OF GENESIS
by Nathaniel T. Jeanson, Ph.D.

First printing: August 2013

All Scripture quotations are from the New King James Version.

ISBN: 978-1-935587-34-7

Please visit our website for other books and resources: www.icr.org

Printed in the United States of America.

TABLE OF CONTENTS

FOREWORD

As any serious student of Scripture knows, the Bible has immense complexity and multiple layers of information, inspired by the single mind and purpose of the Triune Godhead. Through the written Word, God speaks to His creation—especially to those for whom He gave His Son, the great second Person of the Godhead, Jesus the Christ.

The gospel message is founded on the book of Genesis. Without a keen understanding of these beginnings, much of the majesty and wonder of the "good news" is lost in a casual reading. Indeed, the treasures of what God did on our behalf can get lost amid the sweep of history.

Dr. Nathaniel Jeanson has provided a keen analysis of the "map" that God has structured in the lives and events recorded in the early chapters of Genesis. Like any set of clues, the details are very important. Each word and event becomes a literary brick in the path that leads inexorably to the "exceedingly great and precious promises" (2 Peter 1:4) of God's "inheritance...that does not fade away" (1 Peter 1:4).

While the great message of God's grace provided through the Lord Jesus is so clear that even a child can respond in faith (Matthew 19:14), the great treasures of the eternal splendor and beauty of the gospel message can only be grasped by those who "search for her as for hidden treasures" (Proverbs 2:4).

Sadly, some who "dig" around in the scholarship of the world's science and philosophies distort the directions that God has provided. Dr. Jeanson is an impeccable scholar in his own right. He has a clarion warning for those who would obscure the Genesis treasures from others.

Jesus said that those who locate the "treasures" of God's Kingdom would be like "a householder who brings out of his treasure things new and old" (Matthew 13:52). There is much in this little booklet. I would encourage you to read and profit by it.

Henry M. Morris III, D.Min.
Chief Executive Officer
Institute for Creation Research

INTRODUCTION

L ost riches enchant and entice explorers, even to this day. Blackbeard's treasure, Incan gold, European royal gems—the promise of
staggering wealth foments risky behavior and fierce competition.
But an even bigger prize lies within reach of anyone who is willing to
look.

The truths of Scripture are a treasure beyond measure—"more to be
desired are they than gold, yea, than much fine gold….And in keeping
them there is great reward" (Psalm 19:10-11). A quest for biblical meaning is far superior to any hunt for buried gold.

Sadly, the treasures of Genesis 1–11 are lost to many. The scope and
brevity of these opening chapters can puzzle even a careful student of
Scripture. Nearly all of the events in this short section are cosmic or
global in extent, from the creation of the universe to the confusion of
the languages of the entire human population at the Tower of Babel.
The rest of the Old Testament has a distinctly local emphasis, tracing the
rise and fall of Abraham's descendants through Isaac in great historical
and prophetic detail. Genesis 1–11 covers nearly 2,000 years of history
in a section of text that would take less than one hour to read aloud.
In contrast, the next 2,000 years take up the rest of Genesis and all the
other Old Testament books. Clearly, these first 11 chapters represent an
unusual section of Scripture.

Fortunately, God has given us clues for discovering the treasures of
Genesis 1–11. The search doesn't require an archaeological dig or an ex-

pensive expedition. Instead, God placed a unique guide within the text itself that points the way to the immeasurable riches. God's signposts are in the form of literary clues embedded within the biblical text.

An indescribable fortune is at your fingertips. Blackbeard's riches can't compare to this treasure. Let's follow God's literary treasure map as we uncover the untold wealth of Genesis.

∾ 1 ∾

INTERNAL CONNECTIONS:
CLUES TO A UNIFIED WHOLE

Have you ever read a whodunit? If so, you know that the key to solving the mystery is unflinching attention to detail. To an experienced reader, a diverse jumble of clues presents an opportunity and a challenge, not an insufferable obstacle. Vigilant eyes can spot connections where casual readers see only random facts.

The puzzling arrangement of facts in Genesis 1–11 deepens the mystery of these opening chapters. For example, the text of chapter 2 details the events of a single day, but chapter 5 rushes through 1,700 years with a single, concise genealogy. Chapters 6–9 chronicle the events of Noah's year-long Flood, but chapter 10 records another long list of genealogies. Chapter 11 repeats one of the genealogies of chapter 10, and then extends it. At first glance, Genesis 1–11 appears almost haphazard in its presentation.

Upon closer examination, however, a remarkable pattern emerges. Despite their different structures and scopes, these chapters form a cohesive, progressive whole. Numerous events and actions link together and build upon one another.

For example, the first five chapters link via God's primal commands. In Genesis 1:28, God blessed the first human couple, Adam and Eve, by commanding them to "be fruitful and multiply; fill the earth and subdue it; have dominion over the fish of the sea, over the birds of the air, and over every living thing that moves on the earth." In chapter 2, God also commanded them not to eat of the "tree of the knowledge of good and evil" (vv. 16-17). When Adam and Eve disobeyed this prohibition (Genesis 3:1-7), God cursed the means by which they were to realize God's original blessings. By adding pain to childbearing and by adding hard labor to the cultivation of the ground (Genesis 3:16-19), God frustrated the ability of mankind to rule the creation as He originally decreed, a judgment still felt about 1,060 years later at the time of Noah (Genesis 5:29). The first five chapters of Genesis are inextricably linked.

Chapters 3–11 are also connected through God's promise to the serpent. After mankind fell into sin through the deception of the serpent (Genesis 3:1-7), God promised ongoing generational conflict between the offspring of the serpent and the offspring of the woman: "And I will put enmity between you and the woman, and between your seed and her Seed" (Genesis 3:15). This promise was immediately realized just one chapter later. Cain, a child of the devil (1 John 3:10-12), murdered Abel, an offspring of Eve of whom God approved (Genesis 4:1-15). Two chapters after Cain and Abel, we see that "the wickedness of man was great in the earth, and…every intent of the thoughts of his heart was only evil continually" (Genesis 6:5). After God judged this wickedness with the Flood, mankind grew corrupt again (Genesis 11:1-9). Though the devil is not explicitly mentioned in Genesis 6–11, the shadow of Genesis 3:15 hangs heavily over these passages. The promise of ongoing enmity between Satan and humanity resonates throughout this section.

Chapters 5–11 are further connected by the pursuit of a great name. Before the Flood, Noah fathered three sons, one of whom was named Shem (Genesis 5:32), a word literally meaning "name." Shem's genealogy in 10:21-32 precedes the account of a rebellion in which the participants tried to make a great name for themselves (11:1-9). When God intervened, He effectively frustrated the rebels' ability to do so (v. 9). Genesis 11 concludes by tracing one branch of Shem's genealogy down to Abraham (whose name was changed from Abram), to whom God promised a great name (Genesis 12:2). God planned all along whom He would exalt, and no scheme of man or the devil could thwart this.

"Name" also joins Genesis 1–11 to the rest of the Old Testament. Abraham's name did become great; the fate of his descendants occupies the rest of Genesis and the Old Testament. "Shem" has special significance in the larger storyline of the Old Testament.

Genesis 1–11 is not a random collection of incidental events and facts. Instead, God crafted a tightly woven, intimately connected record of the first 2,000 years of history. The content of Genesis 1–11 serves a very specific purpose.

Thus, one of the secrets to the treasure of these opening chapters of Scripture resides in the links among the individual sections. They are not just a collection of muddled details that require us to separate relevant facts from useless incidents. Instead, Genesis 1–11 is an organized, vital component of the priceless riches of Scripture.

The Bible demands a wider lens for discovering the remaining clues. Since all Scripture is ultimately authored by God Himself (2 Timothy 3:16), we might expect the eternal and omnipotent Author of Scripture to have linked passages that no mortal writer could have connected.

He did.

∾ 2 ∾
EXTERNAL CONNECTIONS:
CLUES IN THE REST OF SCRIPTURE

Would you begin reading a novel in chapter 17? Probably not. We know that skilled authors structure each novel with a beginning, middle, and end. The middle and end almost invariably will not make good or complete sense without the beginning. Readers might grasp subplots, but they will lose the subplots' significance and the book's overarching themes without the full context of the entire book.

How many readers of Scripture begin their journey through the Old Testament in Genesis 12? This might seem to make sense, since the promises made to Abraham set the stage for the story of the fate of his descendants, a story that fills the rest of the Old Testament. By comparison, many people see Genesis 1–11 as an isolated, stand-alone block of text with few connections to the rest of Scripture.

Careful re-reading paints another picture. For example, at first glance the significance of the blessing (Genesis 1) and frustration (Genesis 3) of the primal commands of God may seem minor. Genesis references the Curse of chapter 3 in chapter 5 (v. 29), but then seems to fall silent on this judgment. The full scriptural context for these events, however, identifies a further-reaching connection.

The Old Testament alludes to this link with a puzzling passage in the Psalms. When David penned Psalm 8, he referenced God's initial creative act and blessing: "For You have made him [man] a little lower than the angels, and You have crowned him with glory and honor" (v. 5). Then, as though the Genesis 3:17 curse on the ground didn't exist, David wrote "You have made him to have dominion over the works of Your hands; You have put all things under his feet" (v. 6). How could David say "all things" when God made the ground rebel against mankind's rule? Was David using hyperbole?

The author of the book of Hebrews didn't think so. After quoting Psalm 8:6, the writer explained the meaning of David's words: "For in that He put all in subjection under him, He left nothing that is not put under him" (Hebrews 2:8). Clearly, David *did* mean "all things." But does this contradict Genesis 3?

Since Scripture never errs, David must have been prophesying. The author of Hebrews agreed. "But now we do not yet see all things put under him. But we see Jesus, who was made a little lower than the angels, for the suffering of death crowned with glory and honor, that He, by the grace of God, might taste death for everyone" (Hebrews 2:8-9). In His incarnation, atonement, and resurrection, Christ has satisfied part of Psalm 8. The "all things under his feet" will transpire when in the end Christ destroys death. "For He must reign till He has put all enemies under His feet. The last enemy that will be destroyed is death. For 'He has put all things under His feet'" (1 Corinthians 15:25-27).

Christ's victory restores the primal blessing to His own. By becoming our Eldest Brother, Christ lived the perfect life none of us has lived. By dying on the cross, He paid the penalty that we should have borne. By rising from the dead, He secured our justification. By being joined to Him through faith, we become sons of God and joint heirs with Christ. Our inheritance will include part of the dominion we lost at the Fall. In the New Jerusalem, those who are joined to Christ "shall reign forever and ever" (Revelation 22:5).

Christ also seems to restore the "be fruitful" aspect of the primal blessing. When Jesus discussed the Kingdom of God with Nicodemus, He employed very specific language for the entrance requirements: "Most assuredly, I say to you, unless one is born again, he cannot see the kingdom of God" (John 3:3). Jesus didn't say that one must be "transformed" or "enlightened" or "changed." Instead, He used a term with very organic connotations—"born again." Salvation is a new *birth*, and the preaching of the gospel is the means by which others are "born again." Evangelism is, in a sense, spiritual reproduction.

Thus, the primal commands of God connect Genesis 1, 3, and 5 to the rest of Scripture through the events of the gospel.

Many other themes in Genesis 1–11 show up in the remainder of Scripture. God created the tree of life in Genesis 2; the tree appears again in Revelation 22. The serpent tempted Adam and Eve in Genesis 3; Revelation 12:9 identifies the serpent as the devil. God cursed the ground in Genesis 3; God lifts the Curse in Revelation 22:3.

Much of Scripture follows the pattern of a good novel (albeit a true novel). Themes and concepts laid down in the first 11 chapters can be traced through the Old Testament and into the New. Some motifs even appear at the very end, in the closing chapters of Revelation. Genesis 1–11 is intimately connected to the rest of Scripture.

These connections lead us closer to the lost treasure of Genesis 1–11. The clues God wove through Genesis and into the rest of Scripture point the way to the hidden riches. The path to this wealth is becoming clearer.

However, the links between Genesis 1–11 and the rest of the Bible transcend explicitly stated themes. While the opening chapters of Scripture detail some events, they omit others. These omissions and inclusions are deliberate…and they offer another clue in our literary treasure map.

∽ 3 ∽

OMISSIONS AND INCLUSIONS:
CLUES IN THE DETAILS

A good page-turner leaves you "hanging" at the close of each chapter, wondering how the tension will be resolved. Often, multiple subplots are interwoven and told simultaneously so that the reader is left dangling for multiple chapters while the subplots are developed. The intense curiosity created by these omissions forces the reader onward in hot pursuit of the resolution.

Pacing and flow can also create tension through the length of sentences and the level of detail. For example, a fast-paced shootout scene might describe exchanges of gunfire with a rapid succession of short sentences. The speed of delivery matches the speed of the action, leaving you holding your breath in anticipation of the end results. A long, descriptive paragraph in the middle of a gunfight would be odd and out of place, so the author obviously must choose the best format for the writing's purpose.

At first glance, the events of Genesis 1–11 move at an odd, stuttering pace and create little tension. Some sections of human history receive detailed descriptions; others, hardly a passing reference. The main participants appear and disappear with little or no character development. The narrative might seem like a mishmash of random fragments, but a second analysis of the omissions and inclusions in each of these chapters points toward a different conclusion.

The account of Cain and Abel in chapter 4 displays the hallmarks of a purposefully crafted, suspenseful story. In this passage, God recorded their births, and then skipped the story of their childhood and adolescence to jump right to their final, deadly encounter. After describing Abel's murder, God detailed His conversation with the perpetrator, Cain.

Surprisingly, the account excludes any mention of justice for Abel. Though God explicitly approved of Abel's sacrifice, and Christ later called him "righteous" (Matthew 23:35), Genesis 4 records nothing more about Abel after his murder. Surely justice would demand that either Abel be resurrected or that Cain be executed, or both. Justice was not served in this passage. Yet God is perfectly just, and the tension created by this seeming contradiction forces the reader onward in pursuit of the resolution to this dilemma.

The rest of the Old Testament, however, is silent on Abel. The Pentateuch, Joshua, Judges, the Prophets—none of the Old Testament books relieve this tension. In fact, the Hebrew text of the Old Testament seems to heighten the tension rather than diminish it: "'Vanity of vanities,' says the Preacher; 'Vanity of vanities, all is vanity'" (Ecclesiastes 1:2). The Hebrew word translated "vanity" is the same Hebrew word translated "Abel" in Genesis 4. It seems as though the Old Testament writers wanted you to wonder whether Abel's life was lived in vain. The silence on Abel in Genesis 4 after his death and in the rest of the Old Testament leaves you "hanging," wondering whether justice exists for Abel.

This silence is deliberate. When the author of Hebrews reiterated Abel's righteousness (Hebrews 11:4), the writer also explained the reason for the silence on justice for Abel: "And all these, having obtained a good testimony through faith, did not receive the promise, God having provided something better for us, that they should not be made perfect apart from us" (Hebrews 11:39-40).

What was this "something better"?

Christ, the hope of the Old Testament believers. The death of this perfectly righteous God-man had a fantastic conclusion: "Who for the joy that was set before Him endured the cross, despising the shame, and has sat down at the right hand of the throne of God" (Hebrews 12:2). His blood "speaks better things than that of Abel" (Hebrews 12:24), since He was resurrected. Justice does exist for the righteous, but only Christ is perfectly righteous. God will raise Abel, but Abel's own sins needed a just recompense first. The tension and silence of Genesis 4 are signposts to the gospel.

In contrast to the dramatic omissions of chapter 4, Genesis 6–9 swings to the opposite extreme of narrative detail. These chapters on the Flood include not only the fact of Noah's salvation—along with his family and representative pairs of the land-dwelling, air-breathing animals— but also the minute details of this salvation, down to the mathematical dimensions of the Ark. The slow pace of this passage is striking compared to the speed of the preceding chapter. Nearly 1,700 years of history pass in Genesis 5, with hardly a reference to anything besides births and deaths, yet the year of the Flood receives nearly four detailed chapters.

The extreme detail in Genesis 6–9 is deliberate. The New Testament gives a hint as to why: "For if God…did not spare the ancient world, but saved Noah, one of eight people, a preacher of righteousness, bringing in the flood on the world of the ungodly…then the Lord knows how to deliver the godly out of temptations and to reserve the unjust under punishment for the day of judgment" (2 Peter 2:4-5, 9). When Peter warned his audience about false teachers, he reminded them of Noah to illustrate the judgment awaiting such teachers and the hope for those who do not follow their teachings.

Why would Noah's example encourage Peter's audience? Peter reasoned from the greater to the lesser. Before the Flood, the population of the earth may have been in the millions, if not billions. Every single one of these people, aside from Noah and his family, was wicked. If anyone faced dangerous and oppressive adversaries, Noah and his family did. Since his time, no one has faced an entire planet full of wicked people.

The scope of Noah's opposition posed no problem for God's precise judgment and salvation. God knew who was righteous, and He exactly preserved His own. In fact, God even preserved the precise animals that He desired to save. Hence, if God can save Noah out of a sea of wicked people, then surely He can save us.

The extra level of detail in Genesis 6–9 serves to remind the reader that no detail of salvation and judgment is lost on God. He has already calculated how He will save His own and judge His enemies, right down to the last inch of the vehicle by which salvation will be brought. The Ark was perfect in size for the purposes God intended. God knows how to save the righteous and judge the wicked, and God inspired extra detail in the account of the Flood to remind us of this fact.

Thus, one of the keys to the treasures of Genesis 1–11 is a keen eye for omissions and inclusions. Sensitivity to these literary clues reveals the features of a suspenseful and controlled form in these opening chapters. God deliberately chose which facts to provide and which facts to leave out, down to the individual words He selected to record the details.

These observations draw us even closer to the lost fortune of Genesis 1–11. The path to the riches is almost complete. A closer examination of the explicit connections between these chapters and the gospel will reveal yet another clue.

∽ 4 ∾
GENESIS AND THE GOSPEL: A DEEPLY ROOTED PLOT

Stories typically have a central character whose actions and history drive the main plot. Writers deliberately arrange the actions of other characters and the placement of additional subplots to accentuate the primary narrative. The momentum of the main storyline carries the reader forward to the book's conclusion.

What's the main storyline of Scripture? The gospel. Christ's substitutionary death, burial, and bodily resurrection (1 Corinthians 15:1-8) tie the Old and the New Testaments together into one, great salvation story. The gospel is central to Scripture.

Does the gospel trace to Genesis 1–11? The unusual features of this section make it stand out from the rest of the Old Testament. The compression of thousands of years of history, the unusual characters, the global scope—all of these facets seemingly suggest a fundamental disconnect between these opening chapters and the rest of Scripture. However, a careful examination of the different facets of the gospel will unveil a deeply rooted plotline.

The logic of the gospel is founded on the Fall of mankind in Genesis 3. Humans require salvation from sin because Adam, as the ancestor of the entire human race, brought judgment upon all of humanity through his sin in the Garden (Romans 5:12). One man's sin brought condemnation on all.

Paul cited this fact to demonstrate why one man, Christ Jesus, can be the Savior of all who come to Him:

> Therefore, as through one man's offense judgment came to all men, resulting in condemnation, even so through one Man's righteous act the free gift came to all men, resulting in justification of life. For as by one man's disobedience many were made sinners, so also by one Man's obedience many will be made righteous. (Romans 5:18-19)

The events of Genesis 3 set the stage for salvation through Christ alone.

Genesis 3 also foreshadows a future aspect of salvation. Before Adam and Eve sinned, they were both naked, yet unashamed (Genesis 2:25). As soon as they disobeyed God's prohibition, they realized their nakedness and hid from Him in fear (Genesis 3:7-8). God supplied a covering for them, yet His eyes see our nakedness and shame to this day: "And there is no creature hidden from His sight, but all things are naked and open to the eyes of Him to whom we must give account" (Hebrews 4:13).

Only the gospel provides a way of escape from this predicament. Christ bore shame on the cross (Hebrew 12:2). Because of His death and resurrection, "whoever believes on Him will not be put to shame" (Romans 10:11). God's own people will not hide from Him in fear; rather, in eternity "they shall see His face" (Revelation 22:4). Through the accomplishments of Christ, God removes the shame that man brought upon himself in the Garden.

Genesis 3 begins another thread that is not tied up until Revelation. In Genesis 3:15, God promised not only conflict between Satan's and Eve's offspring, but also final victory for Eve's seed: "He shall bruise your head, and you shall bruise His heel." In Hebrew, the verse is literally "He Himself shall bruise your head." God promised that a singular male offspring of Eve would fatally crush the serpent.

God delayed the fulfillment of this promise for the entirety of the Old Testament. None of the descendants of Adam and Eve gained the ultimate upper hand over Satan during that time. On the surface, most of the Old Testament seems to record the triumph of the seed of the serpent, not the seed of the woman.

For example, Satan immediately tried to destroy a righteous seed of Eve (Abel) via Cain's murderous acts (Genesis 4:1-14). God granted Adam and Eve another righteous seed, Seth (Genesis 4:25), to whom was born Enosh, in whose days "men began to call on the name of the LORD" (Genesis 4:26). Yet neither Seth nor Enosh was the promised singular male offspring.

After Enosh, Satan continued his relentless assault on the promise. Every descendant of Adam in Genesis 5 died, except for Enoch, who "walked with God; and he was not, for God took him" (v. 24). Though he was a man who "pleased God" (Hebrews 11:5), he did not crush the serpent. In the days of one of Enoch's descendants, God destroyed the whole earth (except for those on the Ark) because the whole earth had corrupted itself. After the Flood, mankind rebelled again, this time at Babel, requiring another judgment of God (Genesis 11:1-9). After Babel, God chose a man, Abraham, to father a promised nation, but Abraham often stumbled and sinned. Though God miraculously brought Abraham's descendants into Canaan many years later, their recurrent wickedness culminated in their eviction by captivity at the hands of pagan nations (2 Kings 17, 24). Satan seemed to have the upper hand for most of Old Testament history.

Conflict with Satan continued into the New Testament. In fact, Satan actively sought to put Christ on the cross through the agency of Judas: "Then Satan entered Judas....So he went his way and conferred with the chief priests and captains, how he might betray Him to them" (Luke 22:3-4). Christ did go to the cross, and, for a moment, it appeared as though Satan would have the final say. Yet Christ's death was not Satan's victory; it was Satan's deathblow. Christ didn't stay in the grave; He rose again. His death and resurrection defeated the devil (Hebrews 2:14), who will one day receive his ultimate doom in the lake of fire (Revelation 20:10).

Christ fulfilled the promise of Genesis 3:15. Not only did He defeat the devil, He did so as the Seed of the woman. The genealogies of the

Old and New Testaments demonstrate this fact. In Genesis 5, God traced Adam and Eve's lineage through Seth down to Noah and his sons, Shem, Ham, and Japheth. Genesis 11 traces Shem's genealogy down to Abraham. The New Testament immediately continues this theme in Matthew 1, which traces Abraham's genealogy down to Christ. This singular male offspring of the woman is the Seed God foretold thousands of years beforehand.

Thus, Genesis 1–11 sets the stage for the gospel in many explicit and implicit ways. The gospel narrative doesn't commence in chapter 12 with Abraham. It reaches back 2,000 years prior, to the Fall of Adam and Eve.

Together, all the clues we've observed bring us within sight of the treasure of Genesis 1–11. The cohesiveness among these chapters, the connections between these chapters and the rest of Scripture, the deliberate inclusions and omissions, and the special connection between the gospel and these chapters guide us toward the location of the lost riches. One last clue reveals the prize.

∽ 5 ∾
WHY DID CHRIST HAVE TO DIE?: CLUES TO A CONUNDRUM

Movie plots, like book plots, have a definite beginning, rising action, climax, and dénouement. If you walked in on the climax of a movie that someone else was watching, you'd have to ask a series of rapid-fire questions to get caught up on the plot. People tend not to appreciate this behavior, but you'd need it to bring you up to speed on the significance of the part of the story that you just joined.

Many Christians start their study of Scripture at the climax of the story of redemption—Christ's death and resurrection. Unfortunately, some Christians never learn the events leading up to this climax and, therefore, never fully grasp its significance. The solution to this problem is a series of questions that reveals the beginnings of the story of salvation.

Christ's passion culminated a long series of plots and subplots that were built up in the preceding millennia. The purposes Christ accomplished in His death are numerous—taking the curse of the Law for us (Galatians 3:10-13), defeating the devil as the promised Seed of the woman (see chapter 4 of this book), accomplishing forgiveness (Hebrews 9:22), etc. Paul identified one of the most fundamental reasons in 1 Corinthians 15:1-8: Christ died "for our sins."

But why did our sins demand the death of the perfect Son of God?

Romans 3 gives the answer: Christ went to the cross and shed His blood "as a propitiation" (v. 25)—as one turning aside God's wrath. Christ's death satisfied God's holy anger.

Further reflection on this fact raises a pressing question: If the slaughter of God's own precious Son is the only satisfaction for His anger, God's anger must burn hot. Why is God so enraged by sin?

The Old and New Testaments contain several answers to this question. David's confession of sin in Psalm 51 provides the first line of reasoning that justifies the intensity of God's wrath. After David committed adultery and murder, events involving both Bathsheba and her husband, Uriah, David penned a startling statement. Though multiple parties were immediately affected, and though David's sin as king of Israel had consequences for the entire nation, David wrote, "Against You, You only, have I sinned, and done this evil in Your sight" (v. 4).

How could this be true? The rest of the verse explains David's confession: "That You may be found just when You speak, and blameless when You judge." Paul quoted this phrase in the New Testament to justify God's final authority in every matter: "Let God be true but every man a liar" (Romans 3:4). In an ultimate sense, David's sins were only against God because God is the only true lawgiver.

This logic finds its basis in Genesis 1. Because God created the universe and everything in it, including humans, God owns the entire universe, including humans. Therefore, He determines how His property should be used. Adultery and murder are wrong because the Owner of human bodies has decreed that humans should not use their God-given bodies for adultery or murder. The fact of creation explains David's confession.

A second fact explains this confession. Every sin against man is also a sin against God because God embodies the standard by which He judges us. Several passages manifest this truth. At the end of Romans 1, Paul condemns humans for the multitude of sins we commit, and then he intensifies the condemnation by highlighting our hypocrisy: "Therefore you are inexcusable, O man, whoever you are who judge, for in whatever you judge another you condemn yourself; for you who judge practice the same things" (Romans 2:1). Paul contrasts this with the judgment of God: "But we know that the judgment of God is according to truth against those who practice such things" (Romans 2:2). In this context, "according to truth" must mean without hypocrisy, implying that God perfectly keeps the standard by which He judges man. God embodies His Law.

Several other New Testament passages point toward the same fact. The New Testament twice sums up the Old Testament commands, many of which relate to interpersonal relationships:

> "Whatever you want men to do to you, do also to them, for this is the Law and the Prophets." (Matthew 7:12)

> For the commandments, "You shall not commit adultery," "You shall not murder," "You shall not steal," "You shall not bear false witness," "You shall not covet," and if there is any other commandment, are all summed up in this saying, namely, "You shall love your neighbor as yourself." (Romans 13:9)

What do we want men to do for us? How do we love ourselves? We expect just rewards for our good deeds, and we insist on mercy when we err. Hence, we should show justice and mercy to our fellow man. Justice and mercy summarize the Old Testament law.

Justice and mercy also describe God Himself. He is "the habitation of justice" (Jeremiah 50:7), and one of His names is "merciful" (Exodus 34:5-7). In fact, He is love (1 John 4:8). To commit injustice and to refuse to show mercy and love is to reject justice, mercy, and love. To reject justice, mercy, and love is to reject God Himself.

These facts only partially answer the questions of God's intense anger against our sins and why Christ had to die to satisfy that anger. Finding the full answer will reveal the treasure of Genesis 1–11. A little phrase in a familiar verse holds the key: "For all have sinned," begins Romans 3:23. The end of this verse—"and fall short of the glory of God"—solves the mystery of God's wrath and reveals the riches of Genesis 1–11.

∾ 6 ∾
GENESIS 1–11: THE TREASURE

How has mankind fallen short of God's glory? By self-seeking and unrighteous living (Romans 2:7-8). But why does mankind pursue these ungodly ends? Paul identifies the root cause of this behavior in Romans 1—perverted worship. Mankind changes "the glory of the incorruptible God into an image made like corruptible man— and birds and four-footed animals and creeping things" (Romans 1:23). Why? "Because, although [humans] knew God, they did not glorify Him as God, nor were thankful, but became futile in their thoughts, and their foolish hearts were darkened" (v. 21).

The real reason mankind has fallen short of God's glory is because of idolatry. Despite God's obvious revelation of Himself (Romans 1:19-20), man suppresses the truth about God, refusing to thank Him and to glorify Him as the God that He is. Instead, man creates a god in the image of something less glorious than God, such as man himself or nature. Effectively, man tries to "domesticate" God, to bring Him down to a human level. This idolatry leads to behavior that falls short of God's glory.

But why are these crimes so heinous? Why does falling short of God's glory demand such harsh punishment—either the death of the perfect Son of God or the eternal punishment in hell of the unrepentant sinner?

The glory of God displayed in Genesis 1–11 provides the answer. God manifested His glory in the very first words of Scripture: "In the beginning God created the heavens and the earth" (Genesis 1:1). Before the beginning, only God was. He is eternal, without beginning or end. Since only He existed in the beginning, He is not dependent on anyone or anything for His existence or happiness. He is self-sufficient and self-existent. Therefore, He is free to do whatever He pleases.

Humans do not possess these attributes. They have always been dependent upon God for existence, since their existence did not precede God's. Finite and helpless man cannot assail God or remove Him from His supremacy over creation. Man cannot make himself happy apart from God, despite his best efforts spanning millennia of trying. Man cannot change a single atom in the universe without God willing it to be so. God is glorious in His transcendent eternality, self-sufficiency, self-existence, and freedom.

Genesis 1:1 also declares God's omnipresence and omniscience. Because the entire universe derives its existence from God and not vice-versa, God must be outside of time and space. Because God created (Hebrew *bara'*) the universe from nothing, He must have thought of every detail of every particle in every corner in the universe before speaking it into existence. He knows everything.

Man will never eclipse these divine attributes. Individuals are locked in time and space. Improvements in technology have made travel faster, but no one has occupied two positions on the globe simultaneously. These physical limitations severely restrict mankind's knowledge. Satellite technology makes communication easier, as does the global environment in which humans currently exist. But the knowledge each individual possesses is not even a fraction of the knowledge that God possesses.

Man's knowledge of nature is ridiculously inferior to God's omniscient understanding of the universe. We applaud ourselves for discovering the inner workings of the cell, yet we haven't come close to inventing one on our own. Our best inventions are crude imitations of designs that already exist in nature.

God's acts of creation proclaim the glory of His omnipotence and sovereignty. Every time God spoke, the universe responded. The Bible never states, "God spoke, and it failed." For example, when God said, "Let there be light," we read that "there was light" (Genesis 1:3). When

God said, "Let there be a firmament in the midst of the waters, and let it divide the waters from the waters," we read that "it was so" (Genesis 1:6, 8). When God said, "Let the waters under the heavens be gathered together into one place, and let the dry land appear," the text says, "And it was so" (Genesis 1:9). Over and over again the phrase "and it was so" declares the sovereign, unfailing power and rule of God.

Man's attempts to invent, form, or create something pale in comparison to God's. Man has never spoken matter into existence. He must work with the "stuff" that God has already created. Even the processes man uses to engineer God's creation reveal man's limitations. We create prototypes, and then test them to identify the flaws in our initial design. After making improvements, we repeat the process until the design meets our standards. God's designs required no second attempts. He created exactly as He intended the first time, without flaws or mistakes.

The speed of God's acts of creation also declares the glory of God's power. When humans build a skyscraper, it takes a team of workers months to years to construct it, and the end result occupies a tiny fraction of Earth's surface. When God created the entire universe, it took Him, by Himself, only six days.

Genesis 1 reveals God's glorious goodness. The universe would be a hellish place in which to live if God were evil. An eternal, self-sufficient, self-existent, free, omnipresent, omniscient, omnipotent, sovereign being would be a repulsive despot if he delighted in plotting the demise of his subjects.

To emphasize the goodness of God, Genesis 1 records over and over the phrase "and God saw that it was good" (vv. 10, 12, 18, 21, 25), reiterating the glorious virtue of the Sovereign of creation. As if these statements were insufficient to convey the totality of the situation, Genesis 1 concludes God's acts of creation with "God saw everything that He had made, and indeed it was very good" (v. 31). The Ruler of all has been good from the beginning.

Genesis 1 also reveals the glory of God's grace. Though God was the Sovereign Creator of the universe, He graciously delegated some of His authority to Adam and Eve, and He granted them a measure of His creativity in the blessing of childbearing. "God blessed them, and God said to them, 'Be fruitful and multiply; fill the earth and subdue it; have dominion over the fish of the sea, over the birds of the air, and over every living thing that moves on the earth'" (v. 28). God even blessed the animals with the privilege of reproduction (v. 22).

Yet God had no obligation (outside of His own character) to bless mankind and the animals. Neither of the latter had done anything to earn or deserve His favor. God had nothing to thank them for. His own nature compelled Him to bless the dependent fruits of His creativity. Genesis 1 declares the glory of God's grace.

Genesis 2 amplifies His graciousness. When God planted a garden in which to place the man that He created, He did so in a place called Eden, a word that literally means "pleasure." This pleasure garden contained every tree "that is pleasant to the sight and good for food" (v. 9) and a river whose partitions traced the way to lands with precious gems (vv. 10-14).

God also made a woman to help Adam in the Garden. When He did so, God made "a helper comparable to him" (Genesis 2:18), not a misfit or a mistake. Eve was such a perfect creation that Adam spontaneously broke out in poetry (v. 23). Genesis 2 describes a perfect paradise, a testimony to the lavish and glorious grace of God.

God's specific creations reveal His glorious wisdom. "Known to God from eternity are all His works" (Acts 15:18). God chose each creation for a specific purpose, knowing the events that would transpire in the future, and knowing the Scripture that He would inspire thousands of years later. God could have created an entirely different set of things and creatures, yet the ones He chose reflect His unquestionable wisdom. Genesis 1 details these results for our benefit.

For example, we can glimpse the glory of the One who dwells "in unapproachable light" (1 Timothy 6:16) because God created light. We can begin to comprehend the height of His mercy because God created vast reaches of space (Psalm 103:11). We know our dependency upon Christ, "the true vine" (John 15:1-6), because God created plants. We can glimpse the majesty and meekness of His triumphant Son, "the Lion of the tribe of Judah" and the "Lamb" (Revelation 5:4-7), because God created land creatures. God created specific things for specific purposes, much more than is detailed in this short paragraph, yet all of His creations display His glorious wisdom.

God's rest from His acts of creation during the creation week proclaims His glory in a majestic way. The text of Genesis 2:1-3 sounds a loud thunderclap of praise to His incomparable glory. When God completed His creation work, He didn't scramble around the universe to fix poor designs, to educate Himself on parts of the universe beyond His knowledge, or to quell opposition to His reign. Instead, He rested—perfectly in control of all He had done, knowing everything about all He had created, and ruling absolutely in supreme freedom.

No human has ever rested like God did. No human has ever created like God did, and, therefore, no human *could* rest like He did. God's rest is utterly unique and glorious.

The remainder of Genesis 1–11 also magnifies God's glory. God postponed His wrath on shameful man in an act of glorious patience so that man's shame would one day be covered through the redemptive death of His Son. God frustrated the original creation blessings in order to justly punish His rebellious creatures, and then gloriously sent His Son to restore the creation blessings on His reconciled enemies.

God promised a Savior through a Seed, and then gloriously ordained the marriages, births, deaths, and other details of individual lives to fulfill His promise through Mary, despite fierce opposition from the devil. God delayed justice for Abel for 4,000 years and still rendered to Abel what he was due, without fail, in order to gloriously save many sinners through Christ.

God promised to never again send a worldwide flood (Genesis 9:11), and then patiently and gloriously kept His promise for 4,000 years in the face of wicked and hateful enemies. God confused the languages at Babel, and then promised to bless the fractured world through one man, Abraham, making his name great. God ruled through the events at Babel to increase the glory of the New Jerusalem, where "they shall bring the glory and the honor of the nations into it" (Revelation 21:26). God gloriously preserved such a magnificent display of His glory for thousands of years so that we might bask in its glow today. Only God could create a world designed to point to salvation through one man, Jesus Christ.

These demonstrations of God's glory are unspeakably beautiful and stunning. The writer of 2 Chronicles makes this clear when he describes God's salvation of His people as they faced a seemingly insurmountable army. King Jehoshaphat's unusual instructions for the battle used a phrase that many Bible translations miss. "And when he had consulted with the people, he appointed those who should sing to the LORD, and who should praise the beauty of holiness" (2 Chronicles 20:21). Literally, the Hebrew reads that he appointed "ones praising the beauty of holiness."

This phrase has profound ramifications for our understanding of God's glory. "Holiness" translates the typical Hebrew word used for "holy," and it carries the concept of being set apart. For example, God made the seventh day of creation holy by setting it apart from the other six (Genesis 2:3). The Hebrew word for "beauty" in this verse carries the idea of intrinsic beauty and worth, not passing or shallow beauty. Thus, the "beauty of holiness" refers to the intrinsic attractiveness of set-apart-ness.

This beauty is not subjective or limited to cultural context. Why? Because Scripture calls holiness intrinsically beautiful. In addition, Jehoshaphat commanded people to *praise* the beauty of holiness. A beauty so remarkable that a group of singers was dedicated to praising it must be overwhelming and stunning.

God's glory in Genesis 1–11 is holy and, therefore, overwhelmingly beautiful. God is holy in His omniscience, since His omniscience is set apart and unique. No one else knows all things. God is holy in His omnipresence and omnipotence for the same reason. In His freedom, eternality, self-existence, self-sufficiency, justice, mercy, grace, love, forgiveness—in all of His attributes—He is holy, since His attributes are set apart from everyone and everything else. God's holiness extends to every aspect of His being.

His acts are holy. His massive displays of power in creation and in judgment at the Flood are unequaled in Scripture. His accomplishment of eternal purposes at Babel boggles our limited human minds. God's glory in Genesis 1–11 is unambiguously holy and, therefore, unambiguously beautiful.

God's glory is the treasure of Genesis 1–11.

His glory is incomparably delightful, and the opening chapters of Scripture put it on special display. Every recorded detail sounds the heights and depths of His glory in a unique and dramatic way. God's glory in Genesis 1–11 is stunning and unspeakably magnificent.

Yet the beauty of God's glory intensifies our condemnation as sinners. The more we glimpse God's glory, the more it exposes how far we've fallen short of it (Romans 3:23). The wickedness of not glorifying God as omnipotent, omniscient, eternal, free, etc., is magnified in light of the extraordinary and overwhelming beauty of God's glorious attributes. Refusing to glorify God is not just wrong, it is also horrifically ugly.

The glory of God in Genesis 1–11 justifies the wrath of God against sin. Idolatry is a heinous crime because it desecrates God's unspeakably glorious nature. Refusing to submit to the rules of the Owner of the universe is a monstrous offense because the Owner is ineffably glorious. Rejecting God by rejecting justice, mercy, and love is an abominable transgression because God's justice, mercy, and love are indescribably glorious. Refusing to love God with all our heart, soul, and mind (Matthew 22:36-38) is an atrocity because the most glorious Being in the universe is infinitely worthy of His creatures' unflinching and exclusive love. God's intense anger against sin is justified because of the heights and depths of His glory.

However, the glory of God in these opening chapters of Genesis also leads us straight to the heart of the gospel. God's actions when mankind sinned reveal a stunning display of His glory. Surprisingly, when Adam and Eve sinned, God continued His rest from creation, since "the works were finished from the foundation of the world" (Hebrews 4:3). God never second-guessed His activity, tried to create the universe again, or gave any hint that His initial creation was somehow flawed. It was exactly how He designed and planned it from the start.

But why would God rest while man sinned? Though God is not the author of sin, He permitted it to His own praise. How?

The Fall proclaims God's glorious justice. The punishments He enacted at the Fall perfectly matched the crimes committed. For example, the serpent sinned by exalting himself above his created place, and God punished him by bringing him lower than all animals (Genesis 3:14). The serpent tried to destroy mankind; God ordained the serpent's destruction by the hand of his intended victim (v. 15). Eve exalted herself above her created place; God punished her by frustrating her exalted role in helping Adam rule (v. 16). Adam exalted himself above God; God desecrated his office with a curse on the earth that Adam was created to rule (vv. 17-19). God gave the offenders exactly what they were due. With one exception.

Their rebellion also desecrated God's glory. All three were dependent upon God for their existence, and disobedience to His commands represented an egregious slap in His face. Immediate and eternal fire would have been the just punishment for their sins against God. Yet God did not receive the justice due Him in Genesis 3. Why? Because God was simultaneously exercising another aspect of His glorious character.

The Fall also proclaims God's glorious mercy. In judging the serpent, God also ordained the vehicle of the gospel—the "Seed" (Genesis 3:15), which is Christ. God did not permanently deny Himself justice; rather, He postponed His wrath (Romans 3:23-26) and poured it out on Christ many years later. For those who reject Christ, God is still postponing it, but a day will come when He will render "indignation and wrath" to "those who are self-seeking and do not obey the truth, but obey unrighteousness" (Romans 2:8). What God but ours could rest and rule so perfectly through man's sin?

The fundamental elements of the gospel are all revealed in the opening pages of Scripture. The tremendous displays of the glory of God reveal our hearts and expose our idolatry. Yet God's actions at the Fall declare the magnificence of His justice and mercy, which meet in the death and resurrection of Christ. The treasures of Genesis 1–11 are gospel treasures—weighty and heavy, but ineffable and precious beyond compare.

The secrets of Genesis 1–11 are hidden no longer. The lost treasure has been discovered. The literary clues within these chapters have led us to the goldmine.

Or have we missed something?

∾ 7 ∾
COUNTERFEITS AND FORGERIES: THE TREASURE LOST

T he promise of lost treasure is a double-edged sword. The bigger the treasure, the bigger the promise of reward for the discoverer. Conversely, the greater the riches, the greater the temptation to produce counterfeits and forgeries.

Christians sharply disagree on the correct interpretation of Genesis 1–11. Theistic evolutionists ("evolutionary creationists") claim that God used evolution to create the world and that Genesis 1–11 should not be taken literally. Old-earth creationists propose that God did not use evolution but did create over billions of years, and that the days in Genesis 1–11 are figurative at best. Modified versions of both of these ideas are widespread in Christian circles.

Each of these interpretations claims to be true and superior to other interpretations. Proponents of each view assert that they have "discovered" the real meaning of Genesis 1–11 and that they have "resolved" the conflict between faith and science. Advocates market their message in biblical and seemingly believable terms. All of these views reject the interpretation that you have just read in the previous chapters. Which view contains the real treasure, and which views are counterfeits?

Like the clues in our literary treasure map, we also have indicators we can follow to determine this. All counterfeit interpretations of Genesis 1–11 bear the telltale signs of forgery when they are examined carefully in light of the rest of Scripture. The first sign is claiming that the plain reading of Genesis 1–11 leads to internal contradictions. For example, each of the six days of creation ends with "evening" and "morning," yet God doesn't create the sun until Day Four. Therefore, counterfeiters claim that Moses could not have meant literal days for the time span of the events in Genesis 1:1-13.

However, the sun has little to do with the length of the day. The rotation of Earth is the primary process that sets a day's length. As long as there is a light source and a rotating planet, Earth will experience day and night. God created light on Day One, and we know that the earth rotated because there was "evening and morning." In fact, if we let the text speak for itself, Scripture defines "day" very precisely: "God called the light Day" (Genesis 1:5). When there is light, it is "day." It doesn't matter where the light comes from. No contradiction exists among the days of creation in Genesis 1.

All claims of scriptural contradictions are false. Scripture is without error, since the divine Author of Scripture (2 Timothy 3:16) is perfect. Genesis 1–11 is part of the inerrant Word of God, and these chapters do not refute each other. Careful reading of each passage in question resolves apparent disagreements between the texts. "Contradictions" are simply smokescreens that counterfeiters invent to distract the reader from the real riches.

A second sign of counterfeiting is the posing of supposedly unsolvable puzzles. Who was Cain's wife? Did Adam really live 930 years? How could all the animals fit on Noah's Ark? Where did the water for the Flood come from?

None of these puzzles hides the gold of Genesis 1–11. Researchers in each of the major scientific disciplines have discovered plausible answers to each of these questions (visit www.icr.org for over 40 years of articles and technical papers answering these questions). The solutions to these "problems" are readily accessible to anyone with a desire to search. These riddles are simply red herrings to turn the unsuspecting toward useless substitutes.

The Telltale Signs of Forgery

1. Claiming that the plain reading of Genesis 1–11 leads to internal contradictions

2. Posing supposedly unsolvable puzzles

3. Forcing contradictions between Genesis 1–11 and other passages of Scripture

4. Using an unbiblical hermeneutic to determine the meaning of Genesis 1–11

5. Appealing to secular science as an authority on truth

A third sign of counterfeiting is forced contradictions between Genesis 1–11 and other passages of Scripture. For example, some counterfeiters claim that, in their view, the days of creation cannot be literal and that "day" represents eons of time. Counterfeiters even try to make this claim sound biblical by using 2 Peter 3:8: "With the Lord one day is as a thousand years, and a thousand years as one day." Yet this view forces a contradiction with Exodus 20:11, an explanation of the fourth of the Ten Commandments, Sabbath-keeping: "For in six days the LORD made the heavens and the earth, the sea, and all that is in them, and rested the seventh day." If God took eons of time to create, the command to keep a Sabbath becomes unintelligible. Was Israel to work eons of time and then rest an eon? Nonliteral days in Genesis 1 are not biblically viable options. All claims that undermine other Scripture are self-evident frauds.

A fourth sign of counterfeiting is the use of an unbiblical hermeneutic (method of biblical interpretation) to determine the meaning of Genesis 1–11. Some interpreters subtly remove the authority from God's inspired Word with biblical-sounding statements. "Who am I to impose my 21st-century views on the holy writers of Scripture?," they might say. "To understand the real meaning of the text, we need to understand what the author was saying *to the original audience*."

Sounds plausible, doesn't it? After all, we can't assume that the ancients followed the same preferences and practices that we do. For example, in today's scientific world, we insist on reporting scientific measurements to several decimal places. Reporting the value of pi as 3 rather than 3.14 is foreign to the modern scientist's thinking, but may not have been to the thinking of the ancients.

Unbiblical interpreters go beyond appreciating the differences in preference. Proponents of wrong hermeneutics claim that Genesis 1–11 cannot be understood apart from its immediate cultural context, insisting that the text makes sense only in light of ancient Mesopotamian practice. They answer the question "Why is this particular passage in Scripture?" with extra-biblical sources rather than the rest of the Bible. The text of Scripture is not the final authority for these people; the findings of archaeology are.

This is clearly misguided, as previous chapters have revealed. God chose exactly what He wanted in each passage of Scripture, knowing what He would write thousands of years later. He deliberately linked passages in Genesis to the New Testament, even to Revelation.

These links are not coincidental. The Bible is one long Book written by one omnipotent Author. To insist that the meaning of Genesis lies in some Middle Eastern archaeological dig is to mask the true meaning of the text.

The fifth sign of counterfeiting is an appeal to secular science as an authority on truth. The main motivation for this appeal is the antagonism of secular scientists toward Genesis 1–11. For example, modern biologists insist that recent genetic research denies the existence of a literal Adam and Eve. The very idea of a 6,000-year-old earth provokes ridicule and derision from many astronomers and geologists. Even many biblical scholars have wilted in the face of this opposition, accepted the Big Bang and evolution as valid theories, and then forced Genesis 1–11 to fit these predetermined conclusions.

This is short-sighted. Secular scientists—and even some professing Christians who are scientists—begin their search for truth by rejecting the history presented in Genesis 1–11, which makes any effort to harmonize Genesis with their claims futile. Any harmony between the two can stem only from changing the meaning of Genesis 1–11. This leads to many forced contradictions between this text and the rest of Scripture. Appealing to secular science is a sure way to miss the real meaning of the opening chapters of Scripture.

Together, these five signs expose the fraudulent nature of the claims of theistic evolution, of old-earth creation, and of any version in between. If you search the writings of theistic evolutionists and old-earth creationists, you will discover that all five signs characterize their proposed interpretations. Sadly, their claims entice the casual observer with the promise of reward and the sparkle of novelty, despite their worthlessness. Furthermore, their lure distracts from or even hides the real treasure of Genesis 1–11, leaving the duped observer with a double loss once reality sets in.

Tragically, but predictably, these ideas damage and degrade God's glory. For example, one theistic evolutionist declared that evolution expanded her view of God. She explained that evolution implies that God is more like a gardener, planting seeds, observing if they grow, then replanting and trying again when they fail. Do you see the horror of this? Evolution compelled this woman to domesticate God. By treating Him as a gardener, she brought Him down to her level, safe and less glorious—exactly the type of action that Romans 1:18-23 categorically condemns.

Old-earth creation fares only slightly better. By stretching out God's creative activity over millions of years, old-earth creationists tame God's omnipotence and power. Furthermore, old-earth creationists effectively attribute millions of years of death, suffering, carnivory, disease, and bloodshed to God's "very good" creative activity, thereby desecrating His goodness. Whether deliberate or inadvertent, old-earth creation brings God down to the human level.

Theistic evolution and old-earth creation are perilous diversions from the riches of God's Word, and they threaten the discovery of God's glory in Genesis 1–11. The treasures of these chapters are too precious to entertain cheap counterfeits. God's glory is priceless. Genuine alternatives do not exist.

Fortunately, in His kindness, God has given us a readily accessible protection against the gleam of deceptive forgeries.

∾8 ∾
THE TREASURE THAT
EXCEEDS ALL OTHERS

Counterfeit currency is the bane of every banker, investor, and anyone who uses cash. Those who handle large amounts of money on a daily basis are taught to recognize counterfeits quickly. How? By becoming intimately familiar with the real currency.

The best protection against counterfeits to Genesis 1–11 is intimate familiarity with the identity and value of the real treasure of these chapters. How valuable is God's glory? So valuable that God reiterated and proclaimed it over and over again throughout the rest of Scripture. The preciousness of His glory is a message He doesn't want us to miss.

The very words of the Old Testament describe the significance of the glory of God. The Hebrew *kabôd*, translated into English as "glory," carries the idea of "weight" or "heaviness." God proclaimed the massiveness of His glory in the specific words He chose to communicate it.

God also proclaimed the weight of His glory through numerous Old Testament events. For example, when God revealed His glory to individuals, they did not respond with happy awe or a contented sigh. Rather, God's glory overwhelmed them. When God revealed His Law to Israel, He descended on Mount Sinai in a dramatic fashion:

Mount Sinai was completely in smoke, because the LORD

descended upon it in fire. Its smoke ascended like the smoke of a furnace, and the whole mountain quaked greatly. And when the blast of the trumpet sounded long and became louder and louder, Moses spoke, and God answered him by voice. (Exodus 19:18-19)

The people watching responded dramatically to this display of God's *kabôd* (Deuteronomy 5:24):

Now all the people witnessed the thunderings, the lightning flashes, the sound of the trumpet, and the mountain smoking; and when the people saw it, they trembled and stood afar off. Then they said to Moses, "You speak with us, and we will hear; but let not God speak with us, lest we die." (Exodus 20:18-19)

God's glory terrified the people.

When Israel carried out God's commandments to build the Tabernacle, He revealed His glory again. "Then the cloud covered the tabernacle of meeting, and the glory [*kabôd*] of the LORD filled the tabernacle" (Exodus 40:34). The result? "And Moses was not able to enter the tabernacle of meeting, because the cloud rested above it, and the glory [*kabôd*] of the LORD filled the tabernacle" (Exodus 40:35). In fact, God's glory made the Tabernacle holy. "And there I will meet with the children of Israel, and the tabernacle shall be sanctified by My glory [*kabôd*]" (Exodus 29:43). God's glory is weighty and overwhelming.

His holy glory instantly kills His opponents. After Aaron and his sons were consecrated, "the glory [*kabôd*] of the LORD appeared to all the people, and fire came out from before the LORD and consumed the burnt offering and the fat on the altar" (Leviticus 9:23-24). The same fire destroyed two of Aaron's sons. "Then Nadab and Abihu, the sons of Aaron, each took his censer and put fire in it, put incense on it, and offered profane fire before the LORD, which He had not commanded them. So fire went out from the LORD and devoured them, and they died before the LORD" (Leviticus 10:1-2). Why? God proclaimed, "By those who come near Me I must be regarded as holy; and before all the people I must be glorified [*kabad*, the root for *kabôd*]" (Leviticus 10:3). God's weighty glory crushes His enemies.

His glorious acts in history are weighty, unparalleled, and holy. For example, He promised the land of Israel to Abraham and his descendants, and God kept His promise in spite of seemingly impossible obstacles. Though Abraham twice endangered his wife, Sarah, through deception, God preserved their union. When this couple grew old and past the age of childbearing, God granted them a son, Isaac, from whom came Jacob. Despite Jacob's dishonest ways and family conflicts, God gave him 12 sons. God sustained Jacob and all of his family by means of the sinful enslavement and subsequent rule of Joseph in Egypt. Despite twists and turns, God sovereignly upheld His promise.

In Egypt, God protected the nation of Israel from extinction. He saved His chosen leader from infanticide. He dramatically judged pagan Egypt with plagues, and drowned the Egyptian army through the miracle at the Red Sea to spectacularly rescue Israel from Egypt's wicked clutches. God sovereignly preserved His chosen people.

God sovereignly gave the people the land. Over and over, Scripture emphasizes that God was the One who ordained the conquest of Canaan.

> "*I* send an Angel before you to keep you in the way and to bring you into the place which *I have prepared.…I* will send My fear before you, *I* will cause confusion among all the people to whom you come, and will make all your enemies turn their backs to you. And *I* will send hornets before you, which shall drive out the Hivite, the Canaanite, and the Hittite from before you." (Exodus 23:20, 27-28; emphasis added)

After the conquest, Scripture again emphasizes who was responsible:

> So *the LORD gave* to Israel all the land of which He had sworn to give to their fathers, and they took possession of it and dwelt in it. *The LORD gave* them rest all around, according to all that He had sworn to their fathers. And not a man of all their enemies stood against them; *the LORD delivered* all their enemies into their hand. Not a word failed of any good thing which the LORD had spoken to the house of Israel. All came to pass. (Joshua 21:43-45; emphasis added)

Who else has ever performed acts like these? Who else has ever made a specific promise hundreds of years in advance, and then ensured that every word would be fulfilled? Who else has ever demonstrated such sovereign power and might? God's acts in history reveal His simultaneously dreadful and delightful glory.

The rest of the Old Testament and the entirety of the New reveal the weight of His glory. God's patience with Israel's sin, followed by His deliberate judgment through Babylon and Assyria, His return of the exiles to the land of Israel, His sending of the Messiah, His judgment of Christ at the cross—all of God's acts of grace and judgment proclaim the splendor of His nature, the fearfulness of the weight of His magnificence. God's glory is unspeakably beautiful, incomparable, and overwhelming. The treasures of Genesis 1–11 join the rest of Scripture in their precious revelation of the magnificent glory of God. The value of Genesis 1–11 cannot be measured.

The secret to the opening pages of Scripture is manifest. The priceless riches of Genesis 1–11 have been recovered. God's glory is the end of the search, the treasure of treasures, the supreme basis for costly sacrifice and endless praise. God's glory is the treasure that exceeds all others.

NEW FROM ICR

How well do you know the fundamentals of creation? Get the facts with ICR's new hardcover, full-color *Guide to Creation Basics*. This comprehensive 120-page guide, authored by ICR scientists and scholars, is loaded with hundreds of illustrations! To order, call **800.628.7640** or visit **www.icr.org/store**.